The American Idlers

By Cloud Buchholz

Copyright © 2010 by Cloud Buchholz

No People can be bound to acknowledge and adore the invisible hand, which conducts the Affairs of men more than the People of the United States. Every step, by which they have advanced to the character of an independent nation, seems to have been distinguished by some token of providential agency.

George Washington, First Inaugural Address, Apr. 30, 1789

America is a nation with a mission, and that mission comes from our most basic beliefs. We have no desire to dominate, no ambitions of empire. Our aim is a democratic peace -- a peace founded upon the dignity and rights of every man and woman. America acts in this cause with friends and allies at our side, yet we understand our special calling: This great republic will lead the cause of freedom.

George W. Bush, State of the Union Address, Jan. 20, 2004

Table of Contents

Like Drunk You Wrapped Me Up 8

A Good 1st Date.. 9

Left on Purpose 10

I'm Buttoned at the Neck Without a Tie 11

Too Pretty to Eat Unaccompanied 12

Love Poem? 13

Your New Pillow Shams 14

We Should Age 15

I'm a Kindergartner with Safety Scissors 16

Evening in the Summer Time.. 17

Lazy like the Tips of Her 18

Until We're Forming the Same Letters 19

No Love Making Wednesday 20

Two Beer Cans Barely Touching 21

Bandages 22

Your Earrings on My Windowsill 24

Sunday Evening on the Front Steps.. 25

Tuesday... 26

Spilling Towards the Low Point of the Mattress................... 27

The Love Song of 28

The Only Rule is Don't Be Boring 33

Being Single 34

In This Houseful of Other Things 35

I Have About 100 Pairs of Pajamas	36
I Think We All Agree, the Past is Over	37
Singular	38
Like a Girl Walking Past Construction Workers	39
Sorry is the Kool-Aid of Human Emotions	41
Untitled	42
Untitled	43
Discovery	45
Wednesday	46
Until the Mosquitoes Turn Me Home	47
The Third Heaven	48
I. the death of a thief after sunrise	48
II. a day the east wind blows	52
Weary Time	54
Following April	55
A Series of Commas	56
Untitled	57
The Height of the Sun	58
A Body	62
Recognize the Cracks in	63
I Have a Light	65
The Preface of My Story	66
3 Days Before Easter	69
I Lost My Last Memory	70

The American Idlers	71
Des Moines, Iowa	78
Untitled	79
A Couple Wearing Fine	80
The Wedding of Julie Elizabeth Bal & Anthony Paul Seiler	81
A Couple in the Lobby	82
Blond in Boots by the Stairwell	83
Untitled	84
Like Someone Splashed Soda Up Against the Wall	85
Dried Orange Slices in Summer Heat	87
The Table was Spread	88
A Polyphony of Conversation	89
South Elevator	90
Accountability Breeds Response-ability	91
Approximating Smoke	93
Untitled	94
Sitting Alone Outside Burger King	95
Untitled	96
Untitled	97
A Waitress at Mel's	98
the eyelash in my hand	99
Tomorrow	100

Like Drunk You Wrapped Me Up

you think in pieces like a Ferrari

parted-out dress

all hiked up my eyes wire

cutters for your nylons spread

eagle on my telephone

line leaving me like a box

of puppies outside a

super market bonding

with grocery bags

3-26-09

A Good 1st Date

I would like to see

you wearing steam

from the shower with your

hair in a towel tossed

back rubbing water

from your eyes half

closed and carefree

4-11-08

Left on Purpose

a tuft of hair

a tier of blond I thimble

around my finger

It falls in stereo

a rudder to your eyes

the blue of which I maim

with blinks

I am no savant, too primal is my touch

too pungent is my smile

like the sombrero I should never wear

4-29-06

I'm Buttoned at the Neck without a Tie

you're sandals and sweatpants
                         your clothes are frozen candy wrappers
                               I pull off piece by piece
the sheets find the wedging
between your toes
                  courting the idea like
                  investing in the Zeppelin
we move together like
sitting on a straw-bottomed chair
until the seat falls through
                  the windows are in bloom
                  so let's break the hinges
                         my hair isn't dead at the roots
                         but like the sidewalk
                         it's the boundary of something
like gripping a stair rail in the dark
the stutter of your foot finding air
                  I like your hair in braids
                  you have a nice neck
                           rules of animal-etiquette like
                           a diagram of a baseball field
I hold my call lean
into myself and say
hello
you say

4-3-06 *For Colleen*

Too Pretty to Eat Unaccompanied

DNA folding back on

itself spontaneous

proteins activate

ORC binding the shape

changing and we one

and one are simultaneous

2-7-08

Love Poem?

sometimes it's good to give

up before she says take me

home

9-6-08

Your New Pillow Shams

there's no sheets to sleep

summer sweating the

leg hairs cling angled

like a spider walking

toward the crotch unseen

and slow stumbling the dog

curls behind your knees with

dreams of bones and puppy

butts

4-18-08

We Should Age

counting backwards how hide & seek starts

the way the blind rub the notches of their watch

or the rusted chair that doesn't close

like the grass that grows on sidewalks and

how the neighbors talk about the grass

that grows on sidewalks

like yellow spotted leaves brown tipped and eaten through

or taking-in commercial breaks between the news

the way dishes dry in the strainer

like the sweat that stains the bottom of a friend's

Notre Dame baseball hat

like the toys we put in boxes

and give away

5-27-08

I'm a Kindergartner with Safety Scissors

watching with a weathered smile

the way your lips curl

around the red of an apple,

I think of you naked

like in the garden of God

my rib's perfect reflection

10-31-05

Evening in the Summer Time

feels like you

lighting me like the orange moon and

a moment's twilight red and cobalt

blue with warm breezes the horizon goes

you come

and me too

4-25-07 *For Jasmine*

Lazy like the Tips of Her

wasted and wanting
a wet towel dead

on the floor I am
too slow to speak just

watching your eyes
blink as you sleep

have you closed them
for me a moment to

keep like the air
we breathe in winter

or the heat of a fevered
forehead pulling back

an open palm of
sweat sometimes

alone I linger at
the door waiting for

your cheek like
the book I can't

put down how silly you'd
say if you knew

8-9-06

Until We're Forming the Same Letters

like last looks

seeing you in the white

dress with Karin and

your brunette roots grown

back "omg you sluts

look hot!!!" the way you burn a camp

fire or swim with ankles and shins

in Lake Michigan I would have

been the Chicago sky watching

you tan but someday damnit

we'll be poetry together smoking

somewhere in the US like

the hookah you painted in Iowa

or Nashville before ladies night

12-11-07

No Love Making Wednesday

she touches her stomach
surviving used babies she

thieves thank you's and
more thank you's they say

that's a good name he got
she hears a dozen

new religions moving her
eyes to the tips

of radio towers like
drunk birds waiting

to migrate her breasts
never got swollen she

thinks he'll notice and
be disappointed

3-24-09

Two Beer Cans Barely Touching

like the bottle

caps collected at

age five you

find her thinking

as you are and

as she was

7-2-06

Bandages

instinctively we breathe

plunging our bodies into motion

before judging the effects

of a lung's worth of air

I bite my nails until they bleed

momentum of my habits

the telephone cuts onions

the idea and the impulse remain

a rabbit came running, came to keep company

the lion was fed and sedated before

it entered the cage

dialog with memory

like jousting lances quick to reach

the reproduction of themselves

back to the original

the ashtrays are brimming

I take my hand away

gently light a cigarette and

watch the smoke sift

inventory of what we find about

the body the force we resist

torrents of tendency

the girl at the counter smiles

I say it's colder now

we touch objects pinned up

in a towel of experience

unity is lost in activity

the mind is impassible

I think we'll manage

we should try and see

I just wanted to say

smoke spirals from my lips

the pressure of gauze

like snow crust

capturing card catalogs of reproductions

a collection of second-hand books

we read and read again

movement originates from a point of rest

comprehension shivers

she reaches out her hand

a helicopter passes overhead

I don't notice

2-27-06

Your Earrings on My Windowsill

I feel like the quiet

breathing of sleep and

stucco walls

white with the windows

drawn on streetlights

gone

soft with

burnt filament

12-12-07

Sunday Evening on the Front Steps

I touch

you like a half

eaten apple drying

in the hand of

a sleeping afternoon

7-2-06

Tuesday

I slammed the door the other day;

a picture frame fell

the corners were cracked. I couldn't rehang it.

A seascape Monet knockoff,

the kind you buy at the boardwalk.

It was nothing special, except that my mother hated it.

The glass was fine, the picture too.

It was just the boarder

that broke.

There was a little rectangle of white

on the sun-stained wall

10-31-05

Spilling Towards the Low Point of the Mattress

I am tired like

the pavement

leading to your door

7-2-06

The Love Song of

I.

another day

aching to eat and breathe

while I wait to take

the ripples from the sea

like all the works of days before

that have peeled paint

and gathered shells along the shore

or mornings with the window in the nook

the smell of apples in the sun

and bananas turning soft and brown

and how I thought of taking one

yesterday before you brought them home

II.

The couch cushions are soft from your hips

and how you lay like a morning stretch

then curl about the house like yellow smoke

the smoke that walks through narrow streets

and throws its empty shoes upon the beach

to count the seashells blue and white and red

so how should I presume to wait
and how should I begin

I took your slippers from the dog
and wiped the teeth marks off
and saved them for when you get home

III.
And there will be time to come
and go from room to room
through empty halls and half
shut doors to wonder do I dare

to turn back and wonder still
if your legs have grown too thin
to descend the stairs

or if you'll have me guide you down
with arms that wrap about you like a shawl

the years digress and malinger
but let us still talk of you and I
and cheap hotels and restaurants and

oyster-shells

there will be time after all
(you have said so yourself)
and I am waiting still

IV.
I have stood in the dooryards
and searched the sprinkled streets
to find you so meticulous

walking the stone paths each to each
you seem almost ridiculous
almost a fool but
that is not what I mean at all

V.
Should I hem the bottom of your white
flannel trousers or fix the part
in your hair or be of use

an easy tool

the tea kettle whistles

and I move to the noise
to pour a glass of something warm

to warm our throat and tongue and arms
and all our indecision

drying by the furnace
with your boots and socks
and melting snow
would you say it has been worthwhile

to know the mornings, evenings, and afternoons
to know them all already
can you say just what you mean
in a smile

VI.
I am tired of counting saints
like sheep to sleep so tired

of the moss that grows in cracks
along the fence or rain
that gathers oil in the street
and pools rainbows for our feet
and the wheels of our cars

I have heard you singing as you sleep
like the yellow smoke that lingers on the beach
but I know you do not dream for me

I have felt you turning in the sheets
and I have counted
the white hairs I have left to grow

if you hear a whisper as I leave
it was only to say goodnight

10-21-07

The Only Rule is Don't Be Boring

I have no declarations of my own

my life has come and gone

in rented homes

one night dreams

and library books

9-30-07

Being Single

she said I would be a great

wing man for Mike

I told her I had never

met Mike

she said it was ok Mike only

liked the ugly women

she said the pretty ones were

bitches but great in bed

I thought

she seemed nice

6-2-08

In This Houseful of Other Things

missing you is like running

out of toilet paper or drinking 12 cans of Coors Light

alone like a good first date that ends

with masturbation or the sweet syrup inside

the plastic wrapper of an Otter Pop tilting

your head back your hands pressing down

on the corners to open the slit but isn't it

more like the porno I've never seen

the end of and I told myself I would never settle

for a love poem but that's what missing you is

like a love poem I keep in my wallet

like a photograph I can't throw out

9-20-08

I Have About 100 Pairs of Pajamas

biting like

an infant at love

and loving I learn

to suckle

or starve

7-2-06

I Think We All Agree, the Past is Over

like standing on tiptoes

or the way winter slows

into spring and how hollow

I am breast to back

like pulling canvas to a frame

with the love I wear on Sunday

or the streets at closing time

wanting the dimple of your elbow

and the warmth that it brings

but it seems (I think it seems)

I open like water pulsing in a drain

holding written resolutions

you have broken

into details this real

3-21-07

Singular

a telephone voice you talk eager

ringing and I a hand sliding the sound

into a pocket to be found

later like nickels in the dryer or

dollar bills crumpled clean am

a familiar voice wafered

to your ear

2-7-08

Like a Girl Walking Past Construction Workers

a new species found in a

trench 4,000 meters below sea

level through a crack in the earth's

crust a carnivorous sea squirt

funnel-shaped and almost clear like

a Venus flytrap tethered to the sea

floor the Tasman Fracture they say

there's just as much to study but

less to find with climate change

and CO2 levels on the rise and I

wonder if in Australia they care

about AIG giving more than 1 million

dollars each to 75 employees the

financial products division focused

on high-risk mortgage-backed

securities or user content rights in

the Facebook terms of service (which

is now revised) or the 70's radical Sara

Jane Olson released from California

prison and her return to being a Minnesota

housewife or the green glass soda bottle

from the Mexican grill that's

reflecting the sun into neon

lines along the windowsill and white

stucco walls where we

wait for a menu and

a place to sit

03-17-09

Sorry is the Kool-Aid of Human Emotions

blanketing

your feet for

warmth you lie

on the floor near

the dog and

the fireplace

7-2-06

Untitled

only $19.95 late

night plus shipping

and handling the channel

without the remote I finger

the phone and fall

asleep

7-2-06

Untitled

I am, and my father was before,

continuing his thread of restlessness and excess

wasting strength on silence and plenty of good beer

                              and that's enough

                              this routine to the end

Explain why we think as we do

with retracted words we rescue

                to speak a minute with you

                to draw back into

                              the capacity of my throat

                              the tapering of my tongue

She lays her hands upon this house

already in silence a testimony

the clouds are drawn to shade them

                          every contour

                          and rendering

We fall to bed and subside

close the lenses of our eyes

        this mattress and our tugging at the sheets

        pulling too tight to discover your thigh

                        passionate, revealing

              something in us stealing away

I listen with half a smile as your feet touch the floor

contempt collecting in the hall sweeping to the door

            to speak a minute with you

            to draw back into

                      another apology

                      or inbred sentiment

Your cheek-bones catch the light

and mark the present hour

5-7-06

Discovery

like a fly caught between a window and its blinds

we know skin when our finger first finds

touch is the force of

lust like numbering snowflakes is a season that covers

the roads are always straight except at the

bend of your elbow or the pocket of a fist though

my hand never moves past the click of your wrist

watch the laces of your shoes before you trip

on the weight of a name or a

question the cracks and cradle holes of a groaning point of

view, with leather gloves and a syringe, the after-lives of little

animals don't burn nicotine but we do

4-23-06

Wednesday

After three years my shoes wore out

I still haven't bought a new pair

I have thick socks the kind just

long enough to keep your ankles

warm she says she'll buy me

a new pair of shoes she says

she wants to I told her

no

11-10-07

Until the Mosquitoes Turn Me Home

I don't mind walking behind cute women
or scraping tape from old posters on sign posts
those few minutes digging the nail in or the eye
like the plastic cup on the counter holding a dollar
in dimes I sprawl like freedom and the west
coast touching your arm your look
like finding ketchup on your napkin "I
don't know," you say "I think so. She's pretty
anyway." Like a book with perfect binding

my America with drawn on eyebrows and lips just so
red the collar kisses she gives stain the skin
you shake your head "I'm not lonely" you say "I'm not
alone anyway and these barstools are comfortable."
The coffee doesn't keep us up, it only warms our hands
"I don't mind this sunrise" "and scrambled eggs" you add
a little cream to your coffee and stir like you're
walking with your hands full
CNN is counting for us in the corner muted
and we don't mind not looking

for water-stained silverware the waitress laid on another napkin
"We could eat with our hands"
"Like animals at 4 AM"

1-31-08

The Third Heaven[34]

For Gary

I. the death of a thief after sunrise[35]

to love like chalk on sidewalks

being flooded by a garden hose

or dust that gathers on shoulders

of closeted clothes we

linger like rocks collecting the sun[36]

in front lawns, outside restaurants,

and shopping malls

waiting for the leaves to fall

in April afternoons

when rain has made

it hard to breathe

(and we sleep on our sides

with our knees)

---

[34] [10-24-07] — [6-14-08] inspired by 2 Corinthians 12:3
[35] Exodus 22:2
[36] Exodus 33:21

did we share half an apple over breakfast[37]

or a slice of toast

or an evening walk with winter coats

have I known you already

have I let your smell linger with mine

days couple

and weeks and years

like casual t-shirts

worn and still worn[38]

"do you have the paper is it Tuesday

will it rain again today

should I wear a jacket red or blue

with a white umbrella and boots

there's room for two if you stay

close" and slouch a little

everyday

---

[37] Genesis 3:3
[38] 2 Corinthians 5:4

"is the coffee ready

have you fed the cats

are we out of milk

and clean spoons"

"why is it always so cold in this house

we never will be warm enough[39]

now" wrapped in

remnants like the dew mist

that doesn't wait[40]

like the first ripe fruit

shaken from the branch

into the mouth[41]

or the days we live in context

do we love the same after sunrise

in the evening do we steal away

have I known you already

have I felt your heels curved edge like

---

[39] Haggai 1:6
[40] Micah 5:7
[41] Nahum 3:12

a bag that hangs on a shoulder

or the blue veins in your neck when you run

to love like

crumbs collecting in the

corners of the kitchen floor

or pocketed receipts you are

the perfume of your hair

in a crowded room or passing

in a walk and those days before

half shut doors and

open beds we chase

minutes framed in glass

hanging in the hall like

dry stems of grass living

in the cracks of rocks[42]

rain waits for us in its season

fruit waits for us in its tree[43]

---

[42] Obadiah 1:13,18
[43] Leviticus 26:4

on every high hill and under every spreading

tree we are born

as sparks flying upward[44]

again and

everyday "I am

and there is none besides me."

For Karin

II. a day the east wind blows[45]

to love like buried toy soldiers

we find when we're much

older bare ankled in

backyards half

naked and golden-brown waiting

as children chasing

the wind[46] with cupped

hands and eyes

---

[44] Job 5:7
[45] Isaiah 27:8
[46] Ecclesiastes 2:11

closed

have I known you already
have I let your smell linger with mine

like cigarette tips
in ashtrays on the patio table

your remains intermingle
with mine

loving you like
the crackeling of thorns under a pot or
a heart full of nets[47]

---

[47] Ecclesiastes 7:6,26

Weary Time

weary time let me breathe.

the hope of today has come and left.
a shallow slumber is how I rest.

weary time carried by a winter wind let me breathe you in.
open my lungs
    before you pass.
give me hope.
    let me rest.
weary time.
weary time,
 blow hard and swift.

I am waiting for your kiss to pass.

12-24-03

Following April

blossoms

drowsy pink and white

compliment her eyes

unlacing

consigned to capture

a crowded yearning

to construct another year

now falling

like her lips with words

responding

1-29-06

A Series of Commas

I don't know what

day it is and that's the kind

of love we live like collecting

hotel pens from places that we've

never been or when we tell children

goldfish go to heaven (floating

belly up) and they love us

less and now with old age they grow

human ears on mice or

build 5 minute abs before

turning out

the light for bed

2-12-08

Untitled

hearing our name for the first

time and knowing it belongs

to us doesn't keep us

years later

2-5-08

The Height of the Sun

I.

Fish circle the tank

ploughing the brain

numberless and

not exactly comfortable

I flake the surface. They nibble like

small feet for the first time touching

gravel I negotiate time by counting

time spent a dripping faucet filling a sink

that will one day be drained

I once thought death could be captured

in a shoebox buried

in the backyard

he had a freezer in the garage and

the four of us would sit

in lawn chairs and drink fruit flavored soda

I thought he would go to the X-games

he loved Matt Hoffman, loved riding

his first bike had teethed-pedals and he

learned to move his feet fast and when he

wasn't fast enough, how to bandage his shins

connections are collisions of surrender

atoms clash in a symmetry of reaching

to stay close, to move away, to try returning

like a hammer pulling nails from a wall

only to push them back in again

his mother found him one afternoon

in his room holding a shotgun

she reached out

a field touching a shot and fallen bird

the sun navigates the earth as

something felt but never touched

flowers twist their stems

attempting a height beyond cultivation

basic truths are fewer than conclusions

I know that now, but even this will be

recycled

II.

Skin is a story of genealogies and

dusty furniture

sitting with the window open

helps to keep pace with the sun

I hold an appendage of light long enough

to trace the patterns of a flaking self

we played football in the summer with

the heat and one jug of water

I learned to throw a spiral with his

special grip red and gold 49's football

he always wore shoes I ran barefoot

perception is a form of contact influenced by appetite

like picking dark garden tomatoes

and waiting to eat them

the movement of every muscle in slow-motion

can't relate the entire action

like reading newspaper headlines

or ordering groceries over the phone

I stood five feet from the casket

his open eyepits were clayed over

we spoke words without consonants

raked leaves into heaps and bagged them

checked for cracks packed in egg-boxes

cause is the end and origin of change

his mother is slow answering

her eyes are amber cannons

engaged fountains of icicles

a long line of mourners wait

to embrace her, her husband, and

their remaining son

the moment rain becomes snow

she speaks, her tongue striking

something that sounds hollow

when tired the head duck falls back

but never escapes

the currents of the continental self

3-16-06

A Body

of ankles and fingernails
eating their weight

in sugar water and
salt enough to stand

upright like a sign
post or stop light searching

cracker boxes for real
cheddar cheese sweating it

off in the car with the windows
up and the sun shaking

the hand not clutching the steering
wheel too confident

to vomit more water and sleep
the only remedy to hold back

judgment Jesus fasted 40 days and spoke
to Satan about temptation

6-3-08

Recognize the Cracks in

concrete hotel

beds tire like the air inside
my lungs rest

easy she says I
don't mind

to take open space away
from the glass to go home go

ahead sleeping bed like
an open letter I read

alone leaving the same
search following

the same fish no one else
over me a napkin thin wind

take it off
leave it shopping for the

ground will get you nowhere
so late the morning tucked

in tight so late
your chin hooked

to the sky such little things
the sun goes

down day wrinkles
grab your coat come

back into my
walk rest easy lay

your hands like a tongue tasting
a stamp I don't mind

rest easy she says

7-19-06

I Have a Light

like the cigarette
burn in the backseat

of your blue Chevy how
hard you held me in

the afternoon after
school the smell of rem-

embering on your
breath the glass

bottle you hid in
the desk near

the bed catching pieces of
what you left like

picking pennies
from a parking lot

8-10-06

The Preface of My Story

I.
I am the captive of my mind –
>> the walls of thought,
>> and bars of time;
They hold me against myself –
>> they are my crime
as though the fall was my design
>> or the preface of my story.
I stand alone
and gear the gear that once turned me;
>> my pace, like his, too slow to number
Count me as I am, not as any other,
>> framed as no one's image.
I am on the pavement passing
While he lives by stop and go
>> is he wandering,
>> and decaying views of hope?
He laughs to laugh
>> and tickles passing dreams of mine
>>>> with promises.
I sour at their taste
>> and fear the power of his absence
I wash my head, awake, and accept the day.

II.

All time is spent on yesterday --, my prison and still,
        passing my childhood lodgings,
        the garden and the tree,
and the sweet innocence
        I loved and said nothing,
and the rain that fell
I felt but couldn't see,
And I climbed into the tree – branch by branch, to yesterday,
        the preface of my story.
In the clearing of my broken home, I prayed,
          he stayed.
In the neutral swing of drunken fists, she bled,
          we fled.
Back and forth
I lift my arms with pains to reach for heaven,
        the reason to all answers,
concealed inside myself, sheltered in my dreaming.
I am not the same son in the morning
There is no change without control or cause.
I wash my lungs, awake, and breathe the day.

III.

I have myself to blame… not father, home, or
        years that held no time.
Alone, within his raging strain of life –
        I descend,

Taming all the hatred but my own,
breaking limbs and leaves as I fall.
I drag his drunken corpse along the mud,
>> through still and silent moments
>> from freezing drifts of thought,
bless and kiss his bottle to my lips.
Death stands my surest friend,
>> numbs my future
>> breaks me from myself.
I wash my eyes, awake, and realize
I am the captive of my mind –
>> the walls of thought,
>> and bars of time;
They hold me against myself –
>> they are my crime
as though the fall was my design
or the preface of my story.

12-09-05 *For Rick*

3 Days Before Easter

a circle of salt around a snail as

a child I was cruel waiting

to see it cross

the path, bubble, and sink into it's thin

shell, not so different now I

watch a crowd

walk the white

lines of the

crosswalk

3-20-08

I Lost My Last Memory

of you and the winter

we spent parked along the curb

outside my house and how

you kissed the shoulder of my shirt

goodbye in cold morning breath

like pressed flowers shaken

from a book or all the looks

and hands of a crowd

rising up and falling down

8-8-07

The American Idlers

Some are meant to be slaves
and happier that way in
the sentiment of Hollywood
histories on VH1
8 die in a Nebraska mall and
this process of economic law that
educates the few touched
by it is last night's news
Deputy practicing gun draw kills wife
Skateboarders find newborn in dumpster
Model's new ear created from her rib cage
Man beats boy for pink fingernails
Mall Santa says woman groped him 2003
32.7 million prescriptions of Zoloft
Christopher Pittman "is the nation's only inmate serving
such a harsh sentence for an offense committed
at such a young age."
Plumas County spends $20,000 to find lost family
Too much rain in Savannah, Georgia 7 inches in 3 days
Sheila Botelho left her job in the curtains department
for a $5 Powerball ticket purchased in
a Rhode Island convenience store
"At our age, we don't even buy green bananas."
2007 milk prices increased 23.2 percent
Pam Anderson files for divorce after 2 months

Salomon made Paris Hilton sex tape
Reginald Potts, murder suspect, uses Myspace page
to defend himself. Potts listed his mood as "hopeful."
"You don't understand what it takes to be me..."
"I did my best." Maribel Rodriguez says "I'm
deeply devastated with you"
Man dressed in black poses as priest in order
to charge merchandise to church account
David Hasselhoff finally reaches financial,
custody terms with ex-wife
New Jersey becomes first state in 42
years to abolish death penalty
Suit over 'Winnie the Pooh' socks costs school
district $95,000 in legal fees
Redwood Middle School may no longer
require students to wear solid-color clothing
Kevin Federline's lawyer says he'll seek
sanctions against Spears for skipping deposition
Disease-free woman received HIV
treatments for nine years awarded $2.5 million
Teacher accused of sex with student tells
judge she was under 13-year-old's control
"I really thought it just might go away," Peterson
said "I have betrayed your trust" Marion Jones returns
5 medals she won in Sydney
Relay team members asked
to return their medals as well
"This record is not tainted at all. At

all. Period." 756 home runs
"This is it. This is where it
all ends. End of the road. What a
life it was. Some life." Cho Seung-hui 23
years old 32 killed
Orlistat with lipase after a meal
absorbs up to 30% of fat
New Orleans' population reaches
295,450 based on utility hookups
2007 National Oilwell Varco stock +128%
Sgt. Lawrence Hutchins, 23, sentenced to
15 years in the brig for the murder of
Hashim Ibrahim Awad in Hamdania Baby
Jesus equipped with GPS after theft
Clinton donates personal
saxophone to The American Jazz Museum December
18th Charges dismissed in Natalee Holloway case
Jennifer Garner in Oscar de la Renta snags
the Icon Next Door award escaped
tiger kills zoo visitor, injuring
2 others Dotson said he left
a black AK-47-style rifle in the closet so
his ex-wife could protect herself and
the girls against intruders
Barack Obama bust made of
23 lbs of butter
2007 new home sales hit
12-year low 647,000 worst level since

April 1995 builders wait 6.2 months
to sell a completed home northern
right whale spotted off
Brevard County beaches
AMEX oil and gas index up 30 percent in '07
Sergio Baca and Chad Altman, both 22, accused
in Albuquerque Abortion Clinic Fire Dec. 6th Baca's
former girlfriend planned to have an abortion Jim
Leyritz charged after DUI death of
Fredia Ann Veitch, age 30, the mother of
two children ages 5 and 13 Constance
Smith charged with Cruelty to
Children in the 1st Degree www.SitterCity.com had
no comment on their screening process Al
Gore and the U.N. Intergovernmental
Panel on Climate Change awarded 2007
Nobel Peace Prize Mattel CEO, Bob Eckert,
apologizes as company recalls millions
of toys made in China "I'm so sorry
for what I've put you through I
never meant to hurt all of you so
much and I don't blame any one of you
for disowning me I just can't be a burden
to you and my friends any longer You
are all better off without me. I'm so sorry
for this" Letterman and Ferguson return
Wednesday with writers Andres Garcia, 22,
apprehended about 5 a.m. Sunday at

San Diego's San Ysidro border crossing
Staff Sgt. Frank Wuterich, 27, will
face a court-martial on reduced charges
stemming from the killing of 24 Iraqi men,
women and children in Haditha in 2005 a
McDonald's employee, Danielle Miller, 16, gives
birth in bathroom, baby boy Austin is
recovering well Sara Jane Moore, 77, was
released on parole from a federal prison in
California after 32 years Lindsay
Lohan served 84 minutes in Los Angeles
County women's detention center
in Lynwood last month after pleading
guilty to misdemeanor drunken driving
and cocaine charges "I've just snapped I
can't take this meaningless existence anymore I've
been a constant disappointment and that trend
would have only continued. just remember the good
times we had together
I love you mommy
I love you dad
I love you Kira
I love you Valancia
I love you Cynthia
I love you Zach
I love you Cayla
I love you Mark (P.S. I'm really
sorry)" Starbucks shares sank 5.2

percent in afternoon trading on
the Nasdaq $19.34 the lowest price since
2004 Edward Lagrone, executed in
Texas February 11, 6:18 p.m "I
didn't go in there and kill them, but I'm
no better than the people that did. Jesus
is Lord. That's all I have to say." Jeremy
Sisto joins *Law & Order* for
18th season December 31st vandals ransack Robert
Frost's Homer Noble Farm beer bottles and
vomit found in living room San Francisco
zoo reopens 9 days after tiger, Tatiana, mauled and
killed Carlos Sousa Jr., 17, injuring two
others Kulbir Dhaliwal, 23, and Paul
Dhaliwal, 19, Mike Huckabee TV ad features
Chuck Norris for secure borders 8
Massachusetts auto dealerships have agreed
to pay a total $290,000 in penalties after
the state accused the businesses of "asterisk
pricing" "It should go without saying that
the vitality of these constitutional principles
cannot be allowed to yield simply because of
disagreement with them." William Shatner, 76, has
played the role of Priceline.com spokesman for 10
years, 6 years longer than his time spent as Captain
Kirk on *Star Trek* Jamie Lynn Spears appears
on the cover of OK! magazine Dec. 31st
2007 announcing that she is

pregnant the number of consumer bankruptcy filings reached 801,840 a 40% increase compared to 573,203 in 2006 says the American Bankruptcy Institute Tracinda Corp acquires 35% stake in Delta Petroleum Corp for $684 million Kirk Kerkorian named his company after his daughters Tracy and Linda Chief Thomas Warren of the Omaha Police Department called the shooting "premeditated," but said it "appears to be very random and without provocation."

[12-17-07] – [1-03-08]

Des Moines, Iowa

Polaroid postures like tin

can airplanes hanging

from the ceilings of

abandon bar rooms she is

waiting like a hospital

phone or the untied

shoelaces of her son

7-2-06

Untitled

So slow she goes to fold the grass with her

toes. Watching from the window where I wait

for her return, I wonder why she steps

so lightly like the lingering brown leafs

of December. A day ago we spoke

as children small speak fumbling with fin-

gers reaching "Did you hear the moth *tap-tap*

the window?" "No." She says slow rolling to

her side as she turns on the light. "I just--

I thought I heard something upon the glass."

"The tap." "The tap?" "The tap a bug had made

against the glass." "Why would you wake me up

for that? Go back to bed." She seemed to say,

the pillow pressed to half her head. "I am…"

9-20-06

A Couple Wearing Fine

always different they are

standing in line

a pink skirt that doesn't touch the floor

glasses and white pants

coffee two cups by the door

"I woke up considering your silver heart

earrings perky breasts and

"I know" the elevator goes up

laughing shoes shuffle through jarred

fireflies and red fire ants

her eyes his hands

11-19-07

The Wedding of Julie Elizabeth Bal & Anthony Paul Seiler

the groom in the lobby wearing

white like the bride

young with friends he adjusts

his light blue bowtie his smile

of midnight vows, the aisle to walk

and wait she waits white

still with butterflied cheeks each

step to the alter measured

and timed the piano plays

something old and

slow she looks to

his light blue bowtie, his smile her

smile now and the rest

of her life

1-12-08

A Couple in the Lobby

he's open

mouthed with black tennis shoes and

white socks wearing her arm on his

shoulder she's a blue button up

shirt and black socks leaning

her head into his arm not

smiling but not sad watching

the Toshiba slow he taps his

foot she follows too in pink

no-laced shoes laughing

now her chest bounces locked with

her arms crossed her foot touching his shin and

stopping there

4-8-08

Blond in Boots by the Stairwell

blue flannel round face red

cheeks braless with brunette

roots holed jeans at the knee smiling

with her lower lip crossed

arms for cleavage she

checks the center

of her chest

2-26-08

Untitled

I smell the painted

toenails of

my sister before

they do but they

will smell them soon too.

7-2-06

Like Someone Splashed Soda Up Against the Wall

I'll prove
myself soon

enough to
someone like

Bruce Campbell
cameos in

Fargo and
Darkman The

Majestic just
a little

bit of something some
kind of cult

following you
and me even

Stephanie Swift
kisses with her

eyes closed couldn't we
consider strapping

signs to the Golden
Gate Bridge for

Tibet it might mean

we'd meet Richard

Gere and
our lives would

mean something
better like

freedom (and Hannah
Montana topless for *Vanity*

Fair) this feeling of
home like Pope Benedict's[67] ruby

red shoes or the *Narrow Stairs*
we listen to traveling less

from one floor to the
next our knees

creaking just as
much with

Advil

---

[67] Pope Benedict XVI
4-15-08

Dried Orange Slices in Summer Heat

tornado watching we were streets

without wheels kissing faces without

lips fixed in a corner with bottled water

eyes in a basement of cement Grandpa was

gone all the nouns had left his tongue

11-20-07

The Table was Spread

eyes were narcotics of criticism
twisting him with one hand, mind enthralled, liberty deprived

circles under his eyes, bent double, lodging soapbox steps –
threatening speeches spiraled from his nostrils

thrown palely upon the opposite wall –
a wide-awake pattern approaching confinement.

tense muscles restraining bed sheets
commentaries on a combination of nerve ends, cigarettes bludgeoning,

contriving to lock –
precise and unbiased observations of everyday life.

doubted, he, white collar fastened at the throat with
a far-reaching question, held precautionary vigilance

over a thorn-choked garden plot
he turned adrift, creating lines of motion

like a worm or a snarl of wool
unaccustomed to the chilliness of night

11-23-05

A Polyphony of Conversation

like two sleepers rapt in sheets

ready to be ripened when the

morning breaks their dreams

routines the semblance of

what was prior

the quiver of "goodnight"

and the relapse to retire

into what they'll never publish

4-30-06

South Elevator

in case

of fire do

not use

elevator use

stairs

2-28-08

Accountability Breeds Response-ability

when God is something we live

through another TV dinner another

girls gone wild video another

morning paper thrown under the car and

news of Paris Hilton karaoke we

pray but not so

hard just enough to get through

the day and God

seems to listen like the Macy's

weekend sale or the DVD coming

Tuesday and the momentary

buzz between call and caller

ID steals how much of our

lives the preacher is saving

jokes for Sunday and the sanctuary

seats truth becomes a matter of

repetition another TV dinner another

girls gone wild video another

morning between Fruit Loops and

Cocoa Pebbles what would Stephen

Covey do I miss this

country that I've never left we pray

under God and in God

we trust and through God we

live another day of red

white and blue

Approximating Smoke

He wanders with a bag full of clothes
to the closest machine. A thick smell of Clorox rising
from the stained-white, tile-tattered linoleum floor. Air hot,
dry with bleach burning chemicals.
He lets loose his clothes with a five quarter jingle. The machine
starts in. He steps outside with thirsty minutes to waste.
an old wooden bench wrinkled with age
a book's worth of paper humping the curb
a vending machine – Marlboro pressed to its frame
a loitering sign NO PARKING it shouts
He moves slow to the cigarette dispenser examines
every warning, every pack, every label.
With a hand full of change he closes
his eyes remembering the smell, imagining the past,
pressing the button grabbing the red trimmed pack. Against
splintering wood he sits, pulls a cylinder from the box
two fingers to hold it with a fencer's finesse
the smell of his father dancing between fingers as if his soul was
trapped in the plastic wrapped pack.
With every pump of his lung, time folds on itself – years once
stretched twirl lightly in hand.
A chemical kiss with a cigarette tip
like a Father's bedtime good night to his son.
Without a match
the memory fades.

9-07-05

Untitled

my muscles move together
geared pages I pace and retrace
a binding of thoughts curiosity's untethered
I study the lines of your face
faint tracks in the grass like dog-
eared pages I pace and retrace
to find my beginning -- our prologue
wrapped in a worn coat, brushing us in passing
like faint tracks in the grass or dog-
day stories we tell to be telling
just sentimental lunatics craving first draft romance
wrapped in worn coats, brushed by in passing.

in the morning I measure your countenance
kiss the corners of my room
a sentimental lunatic craving first draft romance
but the hope is a sweet perfume
you kiss to the corners of my room.

my muscles move to get her
a binding of thoughts, curiosities untethered

4-16-06

Sitting Alone Outside Burger King

Empty halls of afternoon

sun slow like the calves of old

men waking to wives with thighs

wrinkled white and sagging breasts

slow to rise with breath and eyes

empty still with sleep of nights

younger louder restless hot

sweating smooth with open palms

pressed to dresses orange and green

buttoned half way up with seams

stretched to hips and hard men's grins

going soft

4-10-08

Untitled

use your nuzzle
notice if
unbuttoned we
are so long-lived
"aren't we" to know
we should be but this
condition slow
and bold "weren't we"
to say we love
whose old tradition
now green and brown
with bubble gum smell
put in a purse white and zipped
crossed arms and legs thin
wearing in a paper dress
"weren't we" a book upon a lap
"aren't we" as simple as
this going like anatomy easy
"weren't we" easy
"aren't we"

10-29-07

Untitled

I'm

tempted to talk when

I see your red-vested smile.

Your eyes index my mind

into columns and rows

and so

I stut-ter

in

neatly wrap - ped

pack - ages

of let-ters and sounds.

10-31-05

A Waitress at Mel's

a good poem

is like reading

your nametag or

waiting for your

plastic straws to

put in my cup so

simple the words

you say to so

many everyday the

best kind of poetry

4-19-08 *For Tawnee*

the eyelash in my hand

is yours till we meet again

so don't let it catch the wind

till you close your eyes and send

a wish to kiss me then

11-8-07

Tomorrow

Our eyes

are carpeted

beige for babies

to lay

peacefully.

2-19-08

Made in the USA
Lexington, KY
08 July 2010